HOW TO DRAW MANGA ACTION FIGURES

David Antram

PowerKiDS
press.

New York

Published in 2012 by The Rosen Publishing Group, Inc.
29 East 21st Street, New York, NY 10010

Editor: Victoria England
U.S. Editor: Kara Murray

Library of Congress Cataloging-in-Publication Data

Antram, David, 1958-
 Manga action figures / by David Antram. — 1st ed.
     p. cm. — (How to draw)
Includes index.
 ISBN 978-1-4488-6460-7 (library binding) — ISBN 978-1-4488-6469-0 (pbk.) —
ISBN 978-1-4488-6470-6 (6-pack)
1. Comic books, strips, etc.—Japan—Technique. 2. Cartooning—
Technique. 3. Action in art. I. Title.
 NC1764.5.J3A58 2012
 741.5'1—dc23

                            2011022532

Manufactured in China

CPSIA Compliance Information: Batch #SW2102PK:
For Further Information contact Rosen Publishing,
New York, New York at 1-800-237-9932

Contents

Making a Start

Learning to draw is about looking and seeing. Keep practicing and get to know your subject. Use a sketchbook to make quick sketches. Start by doodling and experimenting with shapes and patterns. There are many ways to draw. This book shows one method. Visit art galleries, look at artists' drawings, see how friends draw, but above all, find your own way.

Use simple shapes at first to try out different action poses.

Perspective

If you look at any object from different viewpoints, you will see that the part that is closest to you looks larger, and the part furthest away from you looks smaller. Drawing in perspective is a way of creating a feeling of space, or of showing three dimensions on a flat surface.

V.P.

The vanishing point (V.P.) is the place in a perspective drawing where parallel lines appear to meet. The position of the vanishing point depends on the viewer's eye level. Sometimes an unusually high or low viewpoint can give your drawing added drama.

V.P.

Two-point perspective uses two vanishing points: one for lines running along the length of the figure and one on the opposite side for lines running across the width of the figure.

Low eye level
(view from below)

V.P.

V.P.

Normal eye level

V.P.

V.P.

High eye level
(view from above)

V.P.

V.P.

V.P. = vanishing point

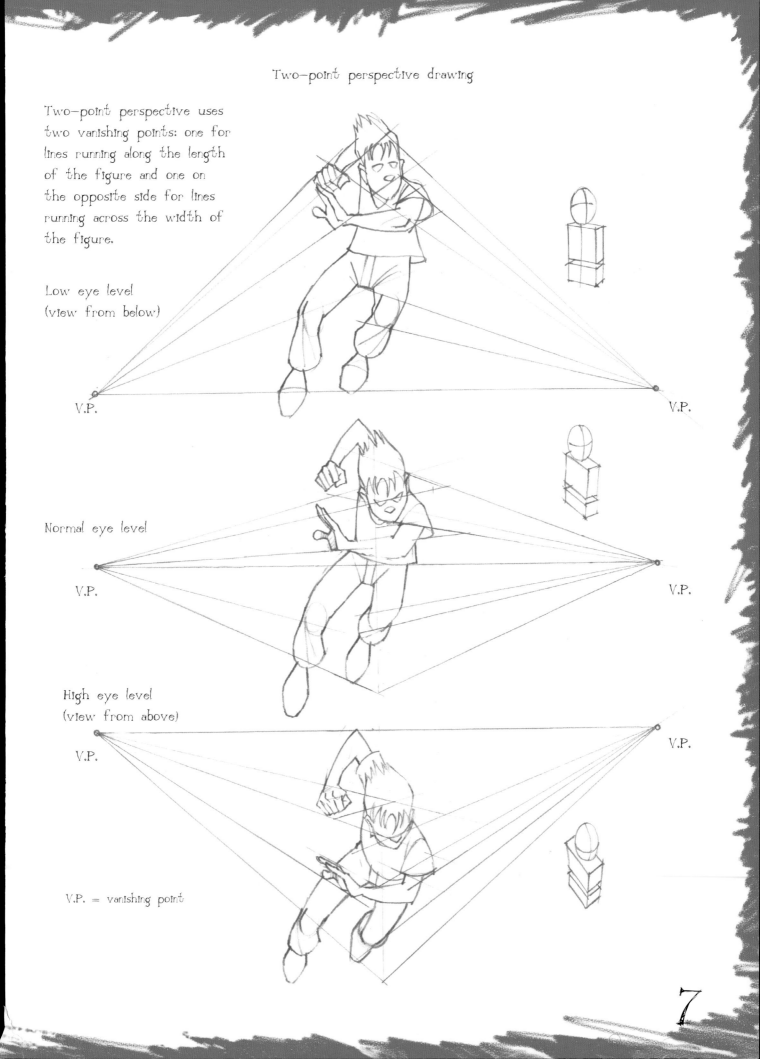

Drawing Tools

Here are just a few of the many tools that you can use for drawing. Let your imagination go, and have fun experimenting with all the different marks you can make.

Pencil

Watercolor pencil

Charcoal pencil

Charcoal stick

Pastels

Finger painting

Black, gray, and white pastel on gray construction paper

Each grade of **pencil** makes a different mark, from fine, gray lines through soft, black ones. Hard pencils are graded as #2½, #3, and #4 (the hardest). A #2 pencil is ideal for general sketching. A #1 pencil is the softest. It makes the softest, blackest line.

Watercolor pencils come in many different colors and make a line similar to a #2 pencil. But paint over your finished drawing with clean water, and the lines will soften and run.

It is less messy and easier to achieve a fine line with a **charcoal pencil** than a stick of charcoal. Create soft tones by smudging lines with your finger. **Ask an adult** to spray the drawing with fixative to prevent further smudging.

Pastels are brittle sticks of powdered color. They blend and smudge easily and are ideal for quick sketches. Pastel drawings work well on textured, colored paper. **Ask an adult** to spray your finished drawing with fixative.

Experiment with **finger painting**. Your fingerprints make exciting patterns and textures. Use your fingers to smudge soft pencil, charcoal, and pastel lines.

Ballpoint pens are very useful for sketching and making notes. Make different tones by building up layers of shading.

A **mapping pen** has to be dipped into bottled ink to fill the nib. Different nib shapes make different marks. Try putting a diluted ink wash over parts of the finished drawing.

Draftsmen's pens and specialist **art pens** can produce extremely fine lines and are ideal for creating surface texture.
A variety of pen nibs are available that produce different widths of line.

Felt-tip pens are ideal for quick sketches. If the ink is not waterproof, try drawing on wet paper and see what happens.

Broad-nibbed **marker pens** make interesting lines and are good for large, bold sketches. Try using a black pen for the main sketch and a gray one to block in areas of shadow.

Paintbrushes are shaped differently to make different marks. Japanese brushes are soft and produce beautiful, flowing lines. Large sable brushes are good for painting a wash over a line drawing. Fine brushes are good for drawing delicate lines.

Ballpoint pen

Mapping pen

Draftsman's pen

Felt-tip pen

Marker pen

Paintbrush

Materials

Try using different types of drawing papers and materials. Experiment with charcoal, wax crayons, and pastels. All pens, from felt-tips to ballpoints, will make interesting marks. Try drawing with pen and ink on wet paper.

Ink silhouette

Silhouette is a style of drawing that mainly uses solid black shapes.

Felt-tips come in a range of line widths. The wider pens are good for filling in large areas of flat tone.

10

Lines drawn in **ink** cannot be erased, so keep your ink drawings sketchy and less rigid. Don't worry about mistakes, as these can be lost in the drawing as it develops.

It can be tricky adding light and shade to a drawing with a pen. Use a solid layer of ink for the very darkest areas and cross-hatching (straight lines criss-crossing each other) for ordinary dark tones. Hatching (straight lines running parallel to each other) can be used for midrange tones.

Cross-hatching

Hatching

Pencil drawings can include a vast amount of detail and tone. Try experimenting with the different grades of pencil to get a range of light and shade effects in your drawing.

Remember, the best equipment and materials will not necessarily make the best drawing. Only practice will!

11

Action Poses

Motion and balance are important aspects to consider in your drawing. Use basic construction lines to create a variety of poses. Then build the drawing up from there.

Exaggerate the curve of the center line to give movement and action to your figure.

Add shading to any areas where light would not reach.

Study real people to see
how their bodies move.

Pay particular attention to
the curve and direction of
the spine and hips.

Use construction lines to
make sure the balance
of the fighting figures
is accurate.

Use circle and oval
shapes to position
the joints.

Keep the drawing quite light and
sketchy at first, until you are confident
that the proportions are right.

Adding Movement

The style and position of the movement lines that you draw can create many different types of fighting movement.

Start by sketching these simple shapes.

Head

Body

Draw an oval for the head and body and smaller ovals for the hands.

Sketch in the arms using straight lines. Add dots to indicate the joints.

Using your construction lines as a guide, sketch simple tube shapes for the arms.

Sketch in the positions of the facial features and hair.

Complete the facial features.

Add circles for the joints.

Add shading and tone to create muscle definition.

14

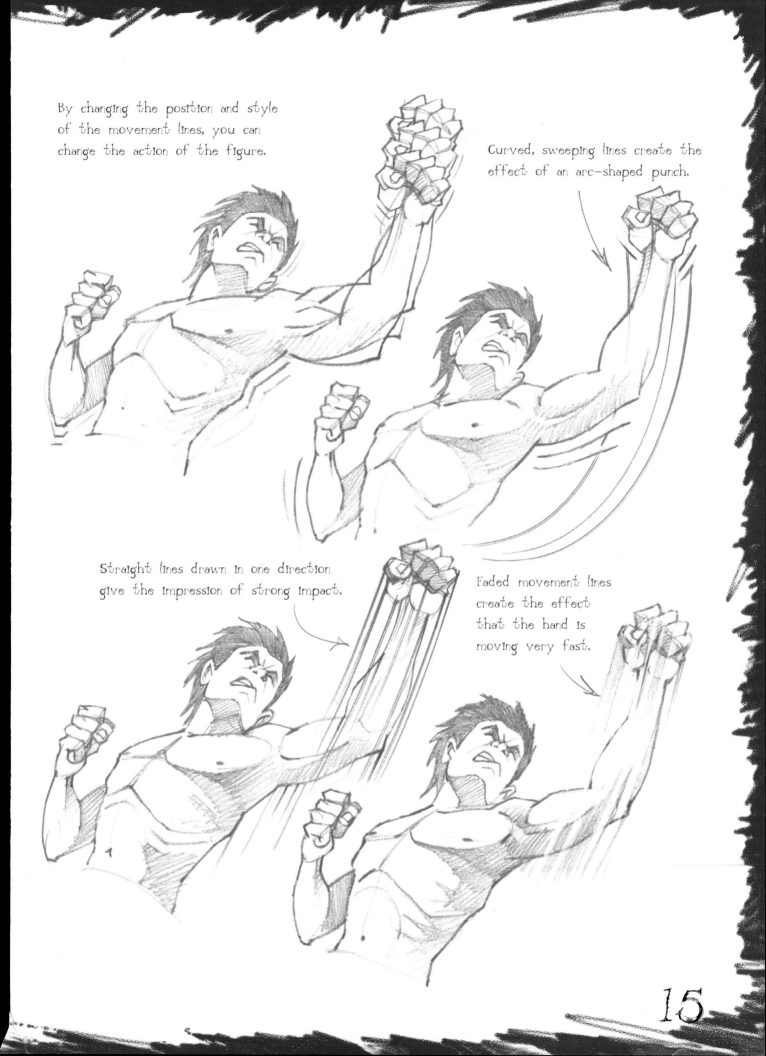

By changing the position and style of the movement lines, you can change the action of the figure.

Curved, sweeping lines create the effect of an arc-shaped punch.

Straight lines drawn in one direction give the impression of strong impact.

Faded movement lines create the effect that the hand is moving very fast.

15

Jumping Fighter

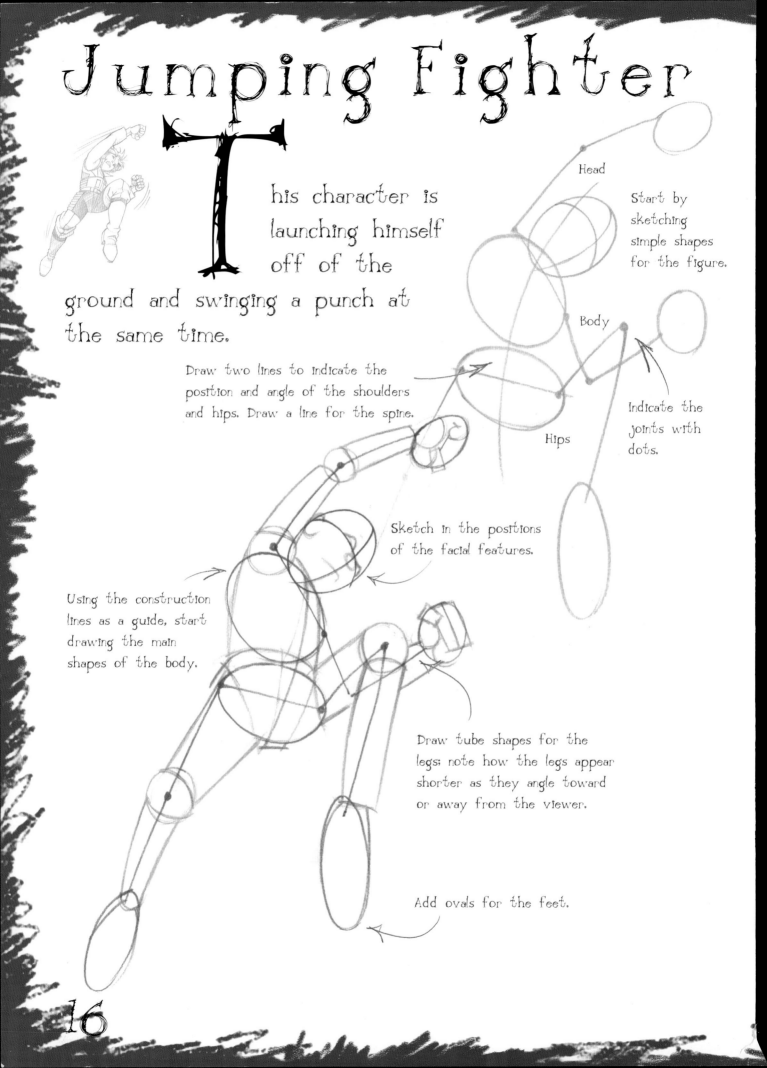

This character is launching himself off of the ground and swinging a punch at the same time.

Start by sketching simple shapes for the figure.

Head

Body

Hips

Indicate the joints with dots.

Draw two lines to indicate the position and angle of the shoulders and hips. Draw a line for the spine.

Sketch in the positions of the facial features.

Using the construction lines as a guide, start drawing the main shapes of the body.

Draw tube shapes for the legs; note how the legs appear shorter as they angle toward or away from the viewer.

Add ovals for the feet.

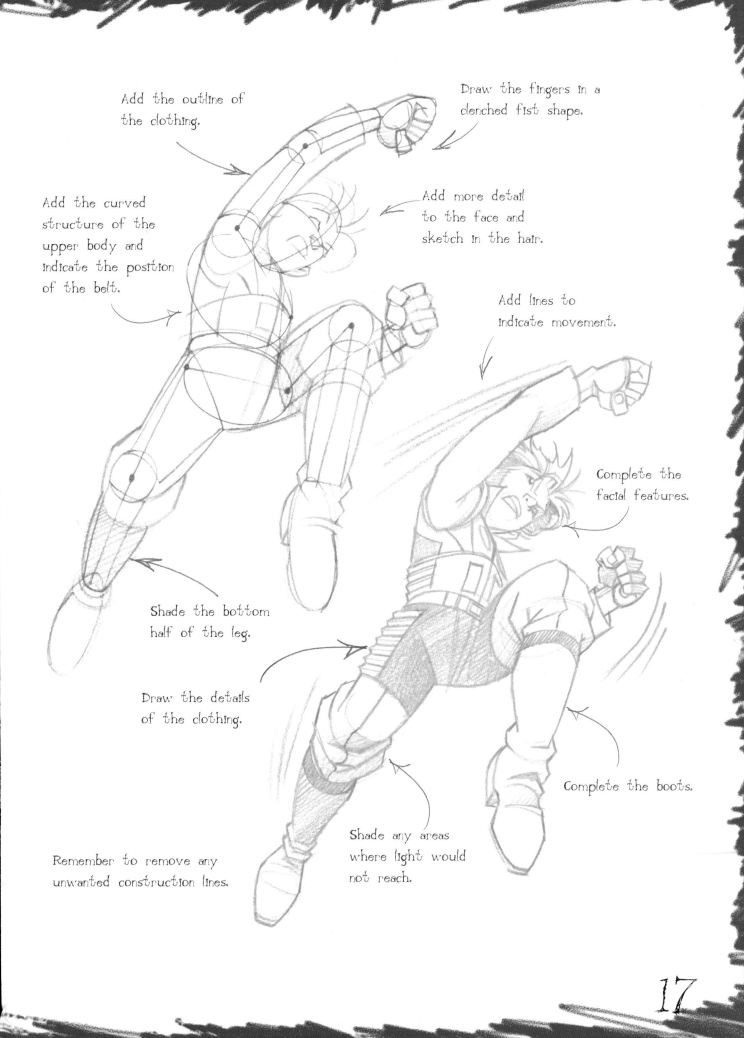

Add the outline of
the clothing.

Draw the fingers in a
clenched fist shape.

Add the curved
structure of the
upper body and
indicate the position
of the belt.

Add more detail
to the face and
sketch in the hair.

Add lines to
indicate movement.

Complete the
facial features.

Shade the bottom
half of the leg.

Draw the details
of the clothing.

Complete the boots.

Shade any areas
where light would
not reach.

Remember to remove any
unwanted construction lines.

17

Martial Arts

Manga figures are often shown in action, performing martial arts moves.

Start by sketching these simple shapes for the figure.

Sketch an oval for the head.

Add an overlapping oval for the body and another for the hips.

Draw the limbs with straight lines.

Indicate the joints with dots.

Add circles for the joints.

Draw oval shapes to position the feet.

Sketch in the positions of the hands using curved shapes.

Sketch in the positions of the headband and nose.

Using your construction lines as a guide, sketch simple tube shapes for the arms and legs.

Draw in the shape of the fingers.

Manga characters generally have very stylized hair. Think about the situation and make the hair fit the scene.

Draw the shape of the clothes, making sure that they go around the body and flare out at the ends of the limbs.

Add spiky hair and start to finish the face.

Draw the toes on the feet.

Add creases to the cloth.

Complete the facial features.

Add shading and tone to the clothes.

Remove any unwanted construction lines.

Complete the feet and ankles.

19

Mecha Giant Robot

This humanoid robot is ready to do battle!

Draw two lines to indicate the position and angle of the shoulders and hips. Draw in a line for the spine.

Draw different—sized ovals for the head, body, and hips.

Head

Body

Draw simple lines for the limbs, adding dots at the joints.

Sketch in oval shapes for the hands.

Hips

Sketch in the shape of the arms and legs, adding circles for both elbows and knees.

Start sketching in the robot's mechanical fingers.

Draw rounded shapes for the feet.

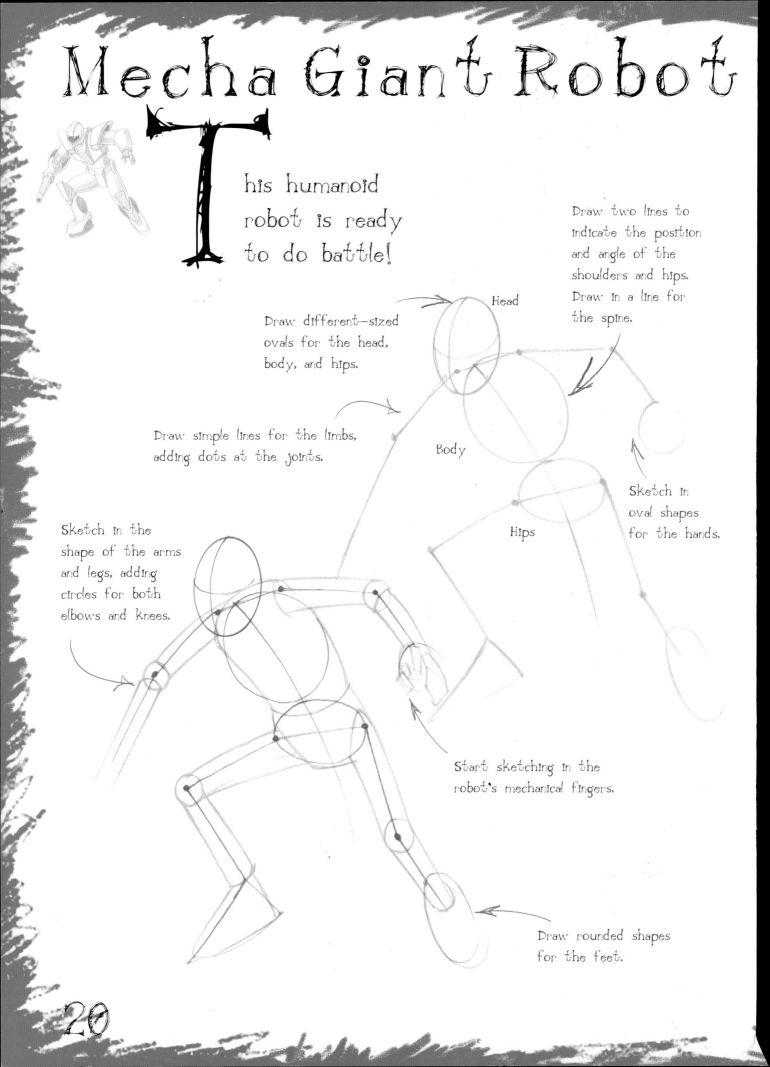

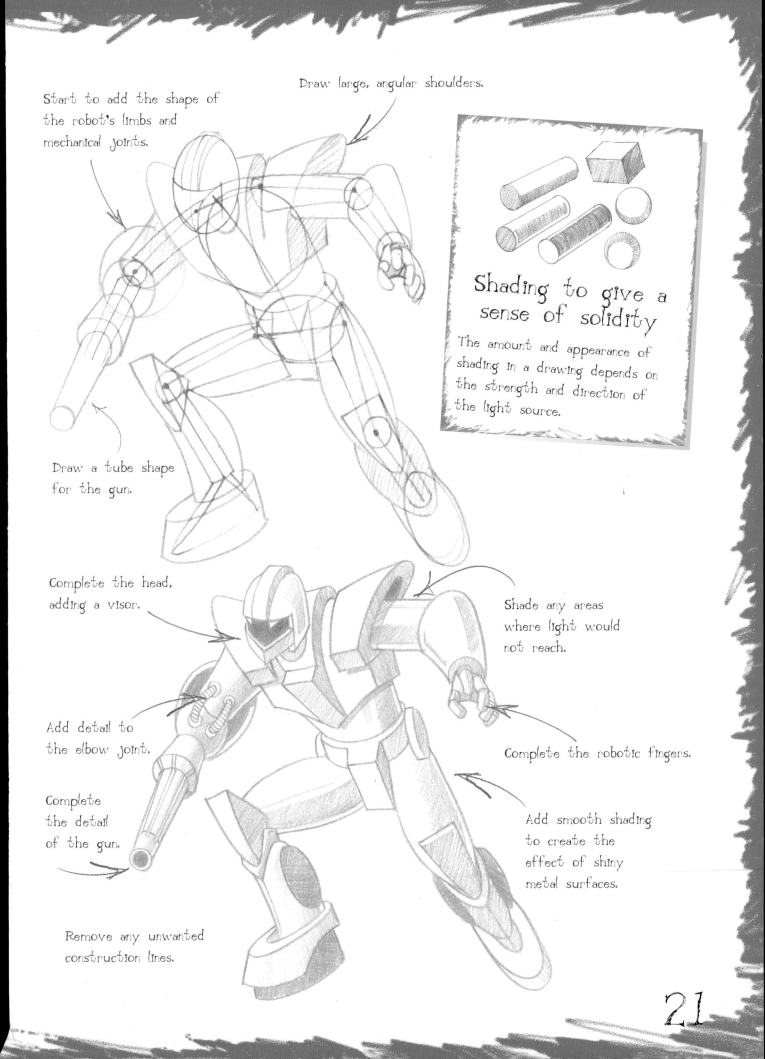

Start to add the shape of the robot's limbs and mechanical joints.

Draw large, angular shoulders.

Shading to give a sense of solidity

The amount and appearance of shading in a drawing depends on the strength and direction of the light source.

Draw a tube shape for the gun.

Complete the head, adding a visor.

Shade any areas where light would not reach.

Add detail to the elbow joint.

Complete the robotic fingers.

Complete the detail of the gun.

Add smooth shading to create the effect of shiny metal surfaces.

Remove any unwanted construction lines.

Action Kick

This character is jumping in the air and doing a powerful high kick. The pose captures a sense of action and excitement.

Sketch in ovals for the head, body, hips, hands, and feet.

Head

Body

Hips

Draw two lines to indicate the position and angle of the shoulders and hips.

Draw straight lines with dots at the joints for each of the limbs.

Fill out the arms and legs using simple tube shapes. The arm that is farther away looks small and the closer leg very large because of the exaggerated perspective.

Indicate the position of the facial features.

Start to add the shape of the hands.

Add more detail to the shape of the feet.

Exaggerated features

Manga characters' facial features have a distinct style and shape. They often have oversized eyes, which help when drawing expressions.

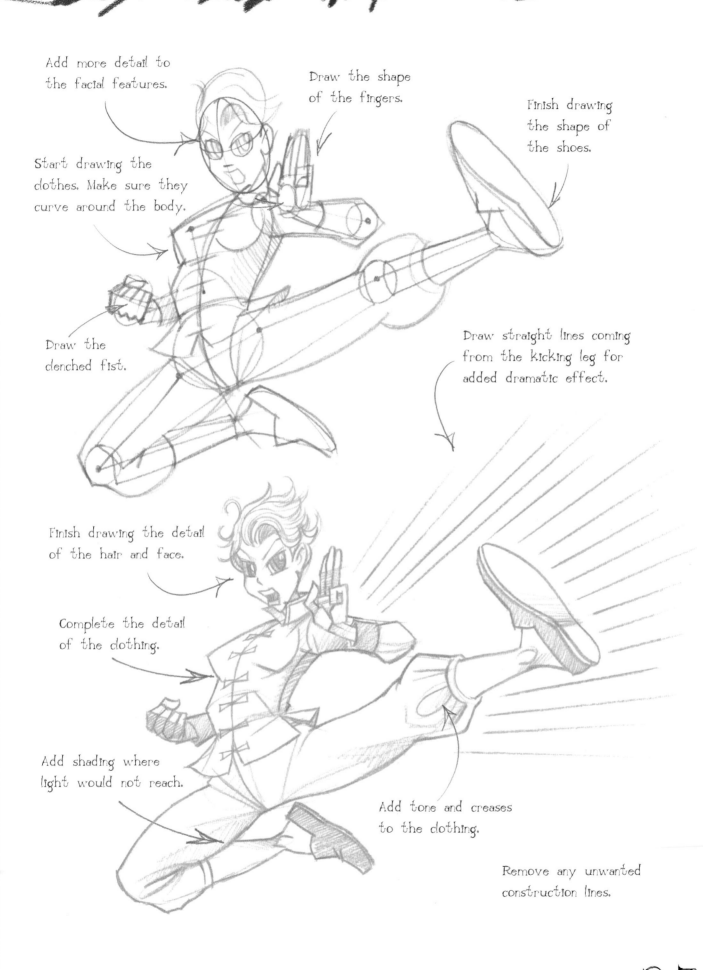

Add more detail to the facial features.

Draw the shape of the fingers.

Finish drawing the shape of the shoes.

Start drawing the clothes. Make sure they curve around the body.

Draw the clenched fist.

Draw straight lines coming from the kicking leg for added dramatic effect.

Finish drawing the detail of the hair and face.

Complete the detail of the clothing.

Add shading where light would not reach.

Add tone and creases to the clothing.

Remove any unwanted construction lines.

23

Defensive Girl

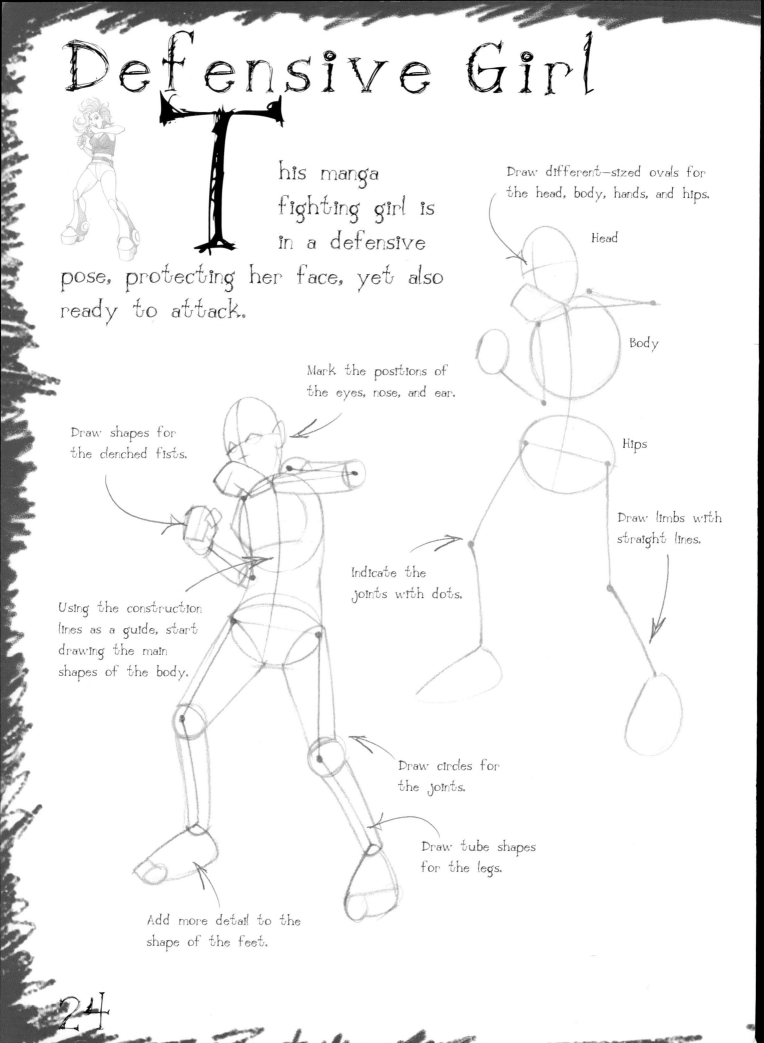

This manga fighting girl is in a defensive pose, protecting her face, yet also ready to attack.

Draw different-sized ovals for the head, body, hands, and hips.

Head

Body

Hips

Mark the positions of the eyes, nose, and ear.

Draw shapes for the clenched fists.

Draw limbs with straight lines.

Indicate the joints with dots.

Using the construction lines as a guide, start drawing the main shapes of the body.

Draw circles for the joints.

Draw tube shapes for the legs.

Add more detail to the shape of the feet.

Sketch the flowing hair.

Add more detail to the face.

Add the curved structure of the upper body and indicate the position of the belt.

Draw the fists.

Sketch the position of the details on the pants.

Finish the detail of the hair using flowing lines.

Complete the face.

Add tone to the clothing by shading.

Finish the belt.

Draw the details of the clothing.

Cropping an image

Choosing a small part of an image and adding a border and a dynamic background can give your drawing more impact. Try drawing straight lines coming out from the figure to create a dramatic effect!

Shade areas like this, where light would not reach.

Falling in a Fight

In battle it can be hard to keep your balance. This character is about to topple over and has a pained expression on his face.

Start by sketching these simple shapes for the figure.

Sketch an oval for the head.

Add an oval for the body and another for the hips.

Add fingers.

Indicate the joints with dots.

Draw two lines to indicate the position and angle of the shoulders and hips. Draw a curved line for the spine (see page 12).

Sketch in the positions of the facial features.

Add circles for the joints.

Draw the main shape of the body, using the ovals to guide you.

Draw the limbs with straight lines.

Draw triangular shapes to position the feet.

Using your construction lines as a guide, sketch the simple tube shapes for the arms and legs.

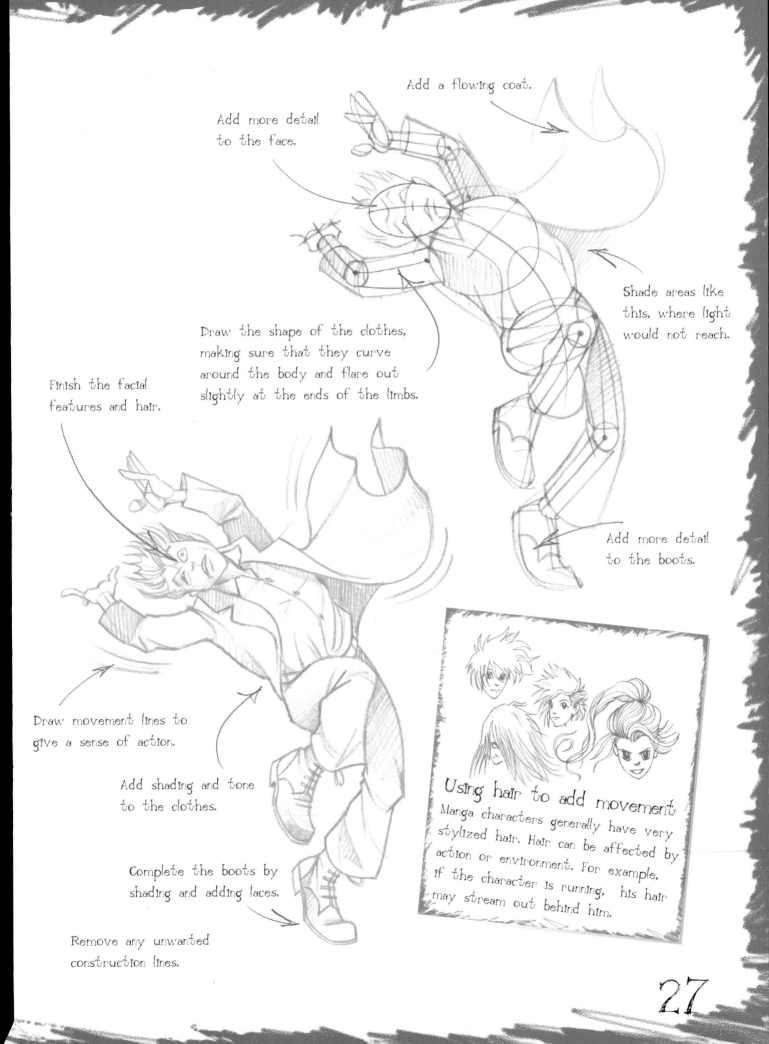

Add more detail to the face.

Add a flowing coat.

Shade areas like this, where light would not reach.

Draw the shape of the clothes, making sure that they curve around the body and flare out slightly at the ends of the limbs.

Finish the facial features and hair.

Add more detail to the boots.

Draw movement lines to give a sense of action.

Add shading and tone to the clothes.

Complete the boots by shading and adding laces.

Remove any unwanted construction lines.

Using hair to add movement

Manga characters generally have very stylized hair. Hair can be affected by action or environment. For example, if the character is running, his hair may stream out behind him.

Fighting Action!

These two manga figures are fighting. One of them is being thrown through the air by a swinging punch.

Draw ovals for the body, head, and hips. Add straight lines for the limbs.

Head

Body

Hips

Draw dots for the joints.

Draw overlapping ovals for the body and hips.

Draw rounded shapes for the hands and feet.

Mark the position of the ear.

Draw simple tube shapes for the arms and legs.

Draw the shapes of the body, using your construction lines as a guide.

Draw circles for joints.

Draw the shape of the hat.

Sketch in the fingers and the outline of the gloves.

Add more detail to the facial features.

Draw the clothing around the body and add shading.

Sketch in the shoes and socks.

Add tone to emphasize the muscles.

Finish off the facial details.

Add shading to areas where light would not reach.

Add movement lines to create a sense of action.

Complete the details of the clothes.

Remove any unwanted construction lines.

Vampire Fight!

A manga hero is tackling a vicious vampire. The expressions on their faces should really show how they feel!

Start by sketching these simple shapes for the figures.

Sketch an oval for the head.

Draw the limbs with straight lines.

Sketch in the positions of the facial features.

Indicate the joints with dots.

Add circles for the joints.

Start sketching in the shape of the fingers and clenched fists.

Using your construction lines as a guide, sketch the simple tube shapes for the arms.

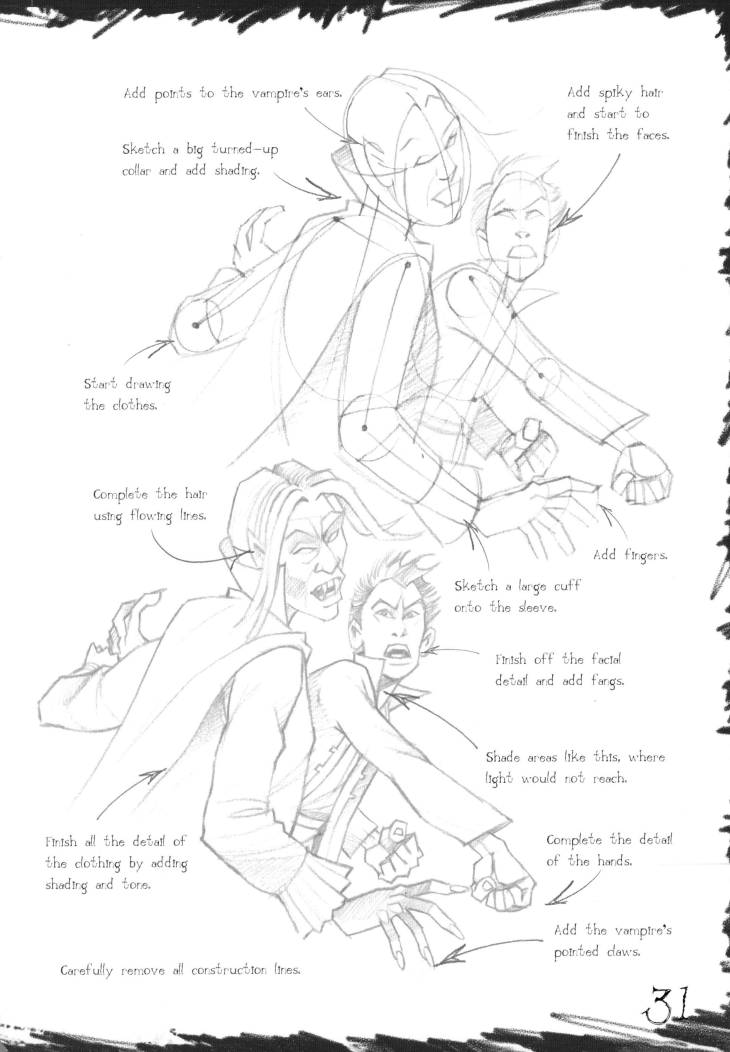

Add points to the vampire's ears.

Sketch a big turned-up collar and add shading.

Add spiky hair and start to finish the faces.

Start drawing the clothes.

Complete the hair using flowing lines.

Add fingers.

Sketch a large cuff onto the sleeve.

Finish off the facial detail and add fangs.

Shade areas like this, where light would not reach.

Finish all the detail of the clothing by adding shading and tone.

Complete the detail of the hands.

Add the vampire's pointed claws.

Carefully remove all construction lines.

31

Glossary

construction lines (kun-STRUK-shun LYNZ) Guidelines used in the early stages of a drawing which are usually erased later.

cross-hatching (KRAWS-hach-ing) A series of criss-crossing lines used to add shade to a drawing.

fixative (FIK-suh-tiv) A type of resin that is sprayed over a finished drawing to prevent smudging. It should only be used by an adult.

galleries (GA-luh-reez) Rooms or buildings that show works of art.

light source (LYT SORS) The direction from which the light seems to come in a drawing.

pose (POHZ) The position assumed by a figure.

silhouette (sih-luh-WET) A drawing that shows only a dark shape, like a shadow.

sketchbook (SKECH-buk) A book in which sketches are made.

vanishing point (VA-nish-ing POYNT) The place in a perspective drawing where parallel lines appear to meet.

Index

Web Sites

Due to the changing nature of Internet links, PowerKids Press has developed an online list of Web sites related to the subject of this book. This site is updated regularly. Please use this link to access the list:

www.powerkidslinks.com/htd/manga/

Titles in This Series

ISBN 978-1-4488-6469-0

9 781448 864690

6-pack ISBN 978-1-4488-6470-6